To Mary Lee Donovan, who kept on laughing.
K. H.

To my dad, J. Robert Lester.
M. L.

First edition 1999

Library of Congress Cataloging-in-Publication Data

Hall, Katy.
Really, really, really bad jokes / Katy Hall ; illustrated by Mike Lester.—1st ed.
p. cm.
Summary: A collection of jokes and riddles, including "smelly" jokes
and jokes in bad taste.
ISBN 0-7636-0695-2
1. Wit and humor, Juvenile. 2. Riddles, Juvenile. [1. Jokes. 2. Riddles.]
I. Lester, Mike, ill. II. Title.
PN6163.H286 1999
818'.5402—dc21 98-42388

2 4 6 8 10 9 7 5 3 1

Printed in Hong Kong

This book was hand lettered by the illustrator.
The pictures were done in watercolor and pen and ink.

Candlewick Press
2067 Massachusetts Avenue
Cambridge, Massachusetts 02140

Really, Really, REALLY BAD JOKES

Katy Hall
illustrated by Mike Lester

CANDLEWICK PRESS
CAMBRIDGE, MASSACHUSETTS

CONTENTS

BAD JOKES
WHAT'S THE EASIEST THING FOR A TRAPPER TO CATCH AT THE NORTH POLE?
A COLD.
WHAT HAS FOUR WHEELS AND HONKS?
A GOOSE ON A SKATEBOARD
WHY DID THE CHICKEN CROSS THE ROAD?
TO GET TO THE OTHER SIDE.
WHAT DID THE NUT SAY WHEN IT SNEEZED?
CASHEW!!
WHY DID EVERYONE THINK THE COOK WAS MEAN?
SHE BEAT THE EGGS AND WHIPPED THE CREAM.
WHAT'S A PIG'S FAVORITE CARD GAME?
PORKER
8

WHY DID THE VAMPIRE HANG AROUND IN HIS PAJAMAS?
HE DIDN'T HAVE A BATROBE.
WHERE DO SHARKS LIVE?
FINLAND.
WHAT DID SANTA SAY TO HIS GARDENER?
HOE, HOE, HOE!
WHERE DO BABY CHICKS LIVE?
CHICK-A-GO.
WHAT KIND OF JOKES DO VEGETABLES TELL?
CORNY ONES.
WHO LIVES IN THE WHITE HOUSE AND RATTLES?
THE PRESIDENT OF THE UNITED SNAKES.
WHY IS AN OLD SCHOOL BUS LIKE A BABY?
BECAUSE IT ALWAYS HAS A RATTLE.

HOW DO YOU STOP CRIME AT A FAST FOOD RESTAURANT?
WITH A BURGER ALARM.
WHAT DO YOU CALL DINOSAUR CHEERLEADERS?
THE PEPTILE SQUAD!
HOW DO HENS AND ROOSTERS DANCE?
CHICK TO CHICK.
REALLY BAD JOKES
HOW DO YOU KEEP AN IDIOT WAITING?
I'LL TELL YOU LATER.
WHY ARE GNUS SMARTER THAN DOGS?
BECAUSE YOU CAN'T TEACH OLD DOGS GNU TRICKS.
WHAT'S THE DIFFERENCE BETWEEN A PIANO AND A FISH?
YOU CAN TUNE A PIANO BUT YOU CAN'T TUNA FISH.
WHEN DOES A HORSE TALK?
WHINNY WANTS TO.

WHAT DOES A TRICERATOPS LIKE TO DO IN THE SUMMER?
GO TO THE DINOSHORE.
WHY DID THE FROG SIT ON THE LILY PAD?
HER COUCH WAS BEING REPAIRED.
LIFEGUARD
WHAT DID ONE MATH BOOK SAY TO THE OTHER?
BOY, HAVE WE GOT PROBLEMS!
MATH
IF YOU BREATHE OXYGEN DURING THE DAY, WHAT DO YOU BREATHE AT NIGHT?
NITROGEN.
A ZEBRA WITH A SET OF DRUMS.
WHAT'S BLACK AND WHITE AND NOISY?
WHEN IS IT BAD LUCK TO BE FOLLOWED BY A BLACK CAT?
WHEN YOU'RE A MOUSE.

REALLY Real
BAD JOKES
WHY DO DOGS RUN IN CIRCLES?
IT'S HARD TO RUN IN SQUARES.
WHY DID THE CHICKEN GO HALFWAY ACROSS THE ROAD?
SHE WANTED TO LAY IT ON THE LINE.
WHAT WOULD YOU BE IF YOU HAD A HUNDRED FEMALE PIGS AND A HUNDRED MALE DEER?
RICH! I'D HAVE TWO HUNDRED SOWS AND BUCKS!
WHY DID THE DUCK CROSS THE ROAD?
IT WAS THE CHICKEN'S DAY OFF.
WHY DID THE CYCLOPS CLOSE HIS SCHOOL?
HE HAD ONLY ONE PUPIL.
WHY DID THE BALD MAN BUY A RABBIT FARM?
HE WANTED TO GROW SOME HARES.

WHAT SHOULD YOU FEED A STAMPEDING ELEPHANT?
ANYTHING IT WANTS!
HOW CAN YOU MAKE YOUR HAIR DANCE?
GET A HEAD BAND!
WHY DID THE MOTHER CALL HER SON BULB?
BECAUSE HE WAS THE LIGHT OF HER LIFE.
WHY DID THE MUSICIAN SPEND SO MUCH TIME IN BED?
HE WROTE SHEET MUSIC.
WHAT WOULD YOU DO IF A GORILLA SAT IN FRONT OF YOU AT THE MOVIES?
MISS MOST OF THE MOVIE.
WHAT DID ONE FLEA SAY TO THE OTHER?
SHALL WE WALK HOME OR TAKE THE GREYHOUND?
POPCORN

WHAT SIDE OF THE CHICKEN HAS THE MOST FEATHERS?
THE OUTSIDE!
WHAT DID THE CHICKEN SAY WHEN SHE LAID A SQUARE EGG?
OUCH!
REALLY REALLY REALLY!!
BAD JOKES
WHY IS BEACH SAND SO WET?
THE SEA WEED.
IF A MAN MARRIES A PRINCESS, WHAT IS HE CALLED?
HER HUSBAND.
IF TWO'S COMPANY AND THREE'S A CROWD, WHAT ARE 4 AND 5?
NINE.
IF YOUR SISTER HAS A WHOLE APPLE AND YOU JUST GOT A BITE, WHAT SHOULD YOU DO?
SCRATCH IT.

WHY DID THE ROOSTER CROSS THE ROAD?
TO PROVE HE WASN'T CHICKEN.
WHAT'S ANOTHER NAME FOR AN EGG COOK-BOOK?
A YOLK BOOK.
COOKING WITH EGGS
SMACK!!
WHAT'S THE BEST WAY TO CATCH A FISH?
HAVE SOMEONE THROW IT TO YOU!
WHY DID THE ANTS RUN ACROSS THE CEREAL BOX TOP?
BECAUSE IT SAID "TEAR ACROSS THE DOTTED LINE."
WHERE DO MOLES GET MARRIED?
IN THE TUNNEL OF LOVE.
NEW

GUESS HOW BAD THESE JOKES ARE...
WHAT DO YOU GET IF YOU CROSS A ROAD WITH A CHICKEN?
TO THE OTHER SIDE.
WHAT DO YOU GET IF YOU CROSS A PIG WITH A KARATE EXPERT?
WHAT DO YOU GET IF YOU CROSS A CAT WITH A VICIOUS FISH?
A PURRANHA!
WHAT WAS THE SMARTEST DINOSAUR?
THE BRAINTOSAURU
WHAT DO YOU GET IF YOU CROSS AN OCTOPUS AND A COMPUTER?
NO ONE KNOWS— BUT IT CAN TYPE 600 WORDS PER MINUTE!

WHAT DO YOU GET IF YOU CROSS A TURTLE AND A PORCUPINE?
A SLOWPOKE.
IF A BUTTERCUP IS YELLOW, WHAT COLOR IS A HICCUP?
BURPLE!
HIC!
PORK CHOPS!
WHAT DO YOU GET IF YOU CROSS A FROG AND AN ELEPHANT?
A REALLY BIG SPLASH!
WHAT DO YOU GET IF YOU CROSS A CALCULATOR AND A CRAB?
12345
SNAPPY ANSWERS.
WHAT DO YOU GET IF YOU CROSS A DENTIST AND A HOOK-AND-LADDER COMPANY?
A FIRE DRILL!

WHAT'S GREEN, HOPS, AND LIVES ALONE?
NO TRESS-PASSING
HERMIT THE FROG.
WHERE DOES LASSIE GO ON VACATION?
COLLIEFORNIA.
Famously Bad Jokes
WHAT BUS CROSSED THE OCEAN?
COLUMBUS.
WHAT DID THE SNEEZING CHAMPION WIN AT THE OLYMPICS?
A COLD MEDAL!
WHERE DOES THE TITANIC GO WHEN IT'S SICK?
TO THE DOCK.
HOW CAN BATMAN TELL WHEN IT'S SPRING?
ROBIN STARTS LAYING EGGS.
18

WHY DID ROBIN HOOD ROB THE RICH?
BECAUSE THE POOR DIDN'T HAVE ANY MONEY!
IF YOU GO INTO A RESTAURANT AND ORDER A BISON STEAK, AFTER THE MEAL, WHAT DOES THE WAITER BRING?
BUFFALO BILL.
WHAT POSITION DID DRACULA'S SON HAVE ON THE BASEBALL TEAM?
HE WAS THE BATBOY
DID HUMPTY DUMPTY HAVE A GOOD SUMMER?
YES, BUT HE HAD A REALLY BAD FALL.
WHY COULDN'T NOAH CATCH MANY FISH?
THERE WERE ONLY TWO WORMS ON THE ARK.
S.S. ARK

Jokes So BAD They're Not Worth Telling

DID YOU HEAR THE JOKE ABOUT THE LIGHTNING?
NEVER MIND- IT MIGHT SHOCK YOU.
DID YOU HEAR THE JOKE ABOUT THE MAGNET?
NEVER MIND- YOU WOULDN'T FIND IT ATTRACTIVE.
DID YOU HEAR THE JOKE ABOUT THE SKELETON?
NEVER MIND- IT'S NOT MEATY ENOUGH FOR YOU.
DID YOU HEAR THE JOKE ABOUT THE BUTTER?
NEVER MIND- YOU MIGHT SPREAD IT AROUND.
MOM
DID YOU HEAR THE JOKE ABOUT THE LAUNDRY?
NEVER MIND- IT'S TOO DIRTY FOR YOU.
DID YOU HEAR THE JOKE ABOUT THE REFRIGERATOR?
NEVER MIND- IT'S TOO COOL FOR YOU.

JOKES IN REALLY BAD TASTE
HOW DO YOU MAKE A RASPBERRY SWIRL?
SEND IT TO BALLET SCHOOL.
WHAT DO YOU CALL SOMEBODY WHO DRINKS 30 CUPS OF HOT CHOCOLATE A DAY?
A COCOANUT.
HOW CAN YOU TELL IF YOU'RE EATING RABBIT STEW?
BY THE HARES IN IT.
HOW DOES CELERY CELEBRATE CHRISTMAS?
IT HANGS UP ITS STALKING.
WHAT DO TOADS EAT WITH THEIR BURGERS?
FRENCH FLIES.
WHAT'S THE RECIPE FOR GREAT ROCK 'N' ROLL?
ANYTHING WITH A GOOD BEET.
WHY DID THE CHEF GO INTO THE PIZZA BUSINESS?
HE WANTED TO MAKE SOME DOUGH.
Recipe

Where do butchers dance?
At the meat ball.
How do you make a meat loaf?
Send it on vacation!
What do you get when you cross a lizard and an outfielder?
A player who catches flies with his tongue.
Why do lions eat raw meat?
They don't know how to cook.
What do you say to someone who likes to eat octopus?
You've got to be squidding!
23

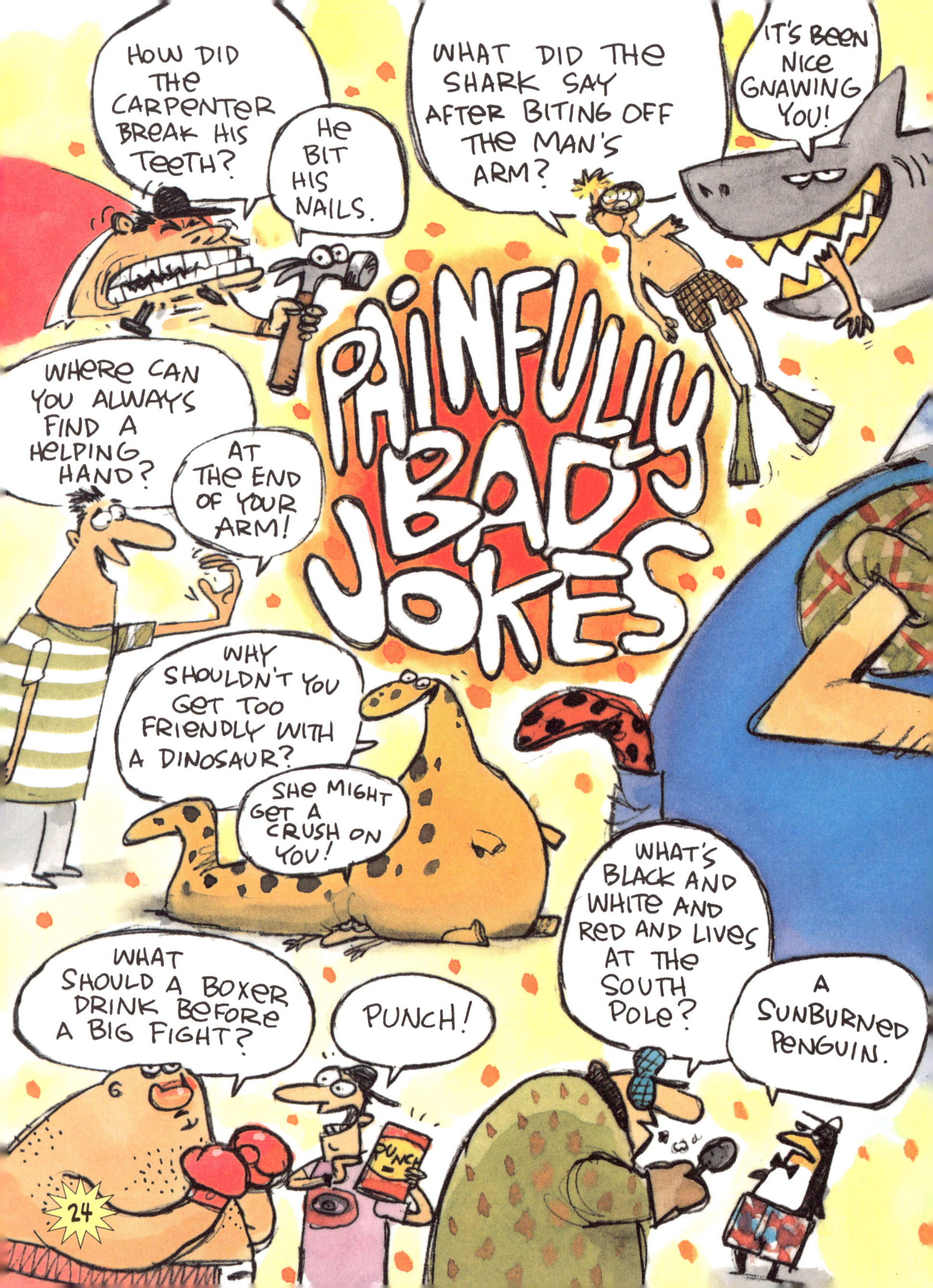
PAINFULLY BAD JOKES
HOW DID THE CARPENTER BREAK HIS TEETH?
HE BIT HIS NAILS.
WHAT DID THE SHARK SAY AFTER BITING OFF THE MAN'S ARM?
IT'S BEEN NICE GNAWING YOU!
WHERE CAN YOU ALWAYS FIND A HELPING HAND?
AT THE END OF YOUR ARM!
WHY SHOULDN'T YOU GET TOO FRIENDLY WITH A DINOSAUR?
SHE MIGHT GET A CRUSH ON YOU!
WHAT SHOULD A BOXER DRINK BEFORE A BIG FIGHT?
PUNCH!
PUNCH
WHAT'S BLACK AND WHITE AND RED AND LIVES AT THE SOUTH POLE?
A SUNBURNED PENGUIN.

WHAT NAIL SHOULD YOU NEVER HIT WITH A HAMMER?
YOUR FINGER-NAIL!
WHAT DO YOU CALL A MAN WHO STICKS HIS HAND IN A LION'S MOUTH?
LEFTY.
WHAT KEY SHOULD YOU SING IN WHEN YOU DROP A PIANO DOWN A COAL MINE?
A-FLAT MINER.
HOW DO YOU PREVENT INFECTIONS FROM BITING INSECTS?
DON'T BITE ANY INSECTS!
WHAT'S THE BEST THING TO TAKE WHEN YOU'RE RUN DOWN?
THE LICENSE NUMBER OF THE CAR THAT HIT YOU!

JOKES SO BAD THEY STINK!
WHAT'S WORSE THAN FINDING A WORM IN YOUR APPLE?
FINDING HALF A WORM.
WHAT KIND OF DOG HAS FOUR LEGS, A TAIL, AND FLIES?
A DEAD DOG.
HOW DO YOU KEEP FLIES OUT OF THE KITCHEN?
PUT A DEAD FISH IN THE DINING ROOM.
WHAT SMELLS THE MOST IN A GARBAGE DUMP?
YOUR NOSE!
WHAT DID ONE EAR SAY TO THE OTHER?
JUST BETWEEN US, SOMETHING SMELLS.

WHY DO GIRAFFES HAVE SUCH LONG NECKS?
THEY CAN'T STAND THE SMELL OF THEIR FEET.
WHAT SHOULD YOU DO IF YOUR NOSE GOES ON STRIKE?
PICKET!
WHAT DID THE JUDGE SAY WHEN THE SKUNK ENTERED THE COURTROOM?
ODOR IN THE COURT!
IF A FOOTBALL PLAYER GETS ATHLETE'S FOOT, WHAT DOES AN ASTRONAUT GET?
MISSLETOE!
WHAT GETS DIRTIER WHEN YOU TAKE A BATH?
THE BATHTUB.
27

Jokes So Bad They'll Kill You!
BANG!
WHAT DO THEY SERVE IN THE CANNIBAL CAFETERIA?
BAKED BEINGS.
WHAT GOES CLUCK, CLUCK, CLUCK, BANG!
A CHICKEN WALKING THROUGH A MINE FIELD.
WHAT HAPPENED TO THE PLASTIC SURGEON WHEN HE STOOD TOO CLOSE TO THE CAMP FIRE?
HE MELTED.
KNOW WHAT THEY CALL SOMEONE WHO HUNTS SHARKS WITH A WATER PISTOL?
STUPID.
WHAT DO YOU CALL A COW WITH NO LEGS?
GROUND BEEF.
WHAT GOES HA, HA, HA, HA, THUMP?
A PERSON LAUGHING HIS HEAD OFF!

WHAT HAPPENED WHEN MOZART AND BEETHOVEN DIED?
THEY DECOMPOSED.
MOZART R.I.P.
BEET HOVEN R.I.P.
WHAT DO YOU GET WHEN A CANARY FLIES INTO A FAN?
SHREDDED TWEET!
WHAT COULD THE MONSTER EAT AFTER GETTING ITS TEETH PULLED?
ITS DENTIST!
WHAT DID MARY HAVE WHEN SHE WENT OUT TO DINNER?
MARY HAD A LITTLE LAMB.
WHAT DO YOU CALL A CANNIBAL WHO ATE HIS MOTHER'S SISTER?
AN AUNT EATER!
WHY WOULDN'T THE WOMAN LET THE DOCTOR TAKE OUT HER HUSBAND'S APPENDIX?
SHE DIDN'T WANT ANYBODY TO OPEN HER MALE.